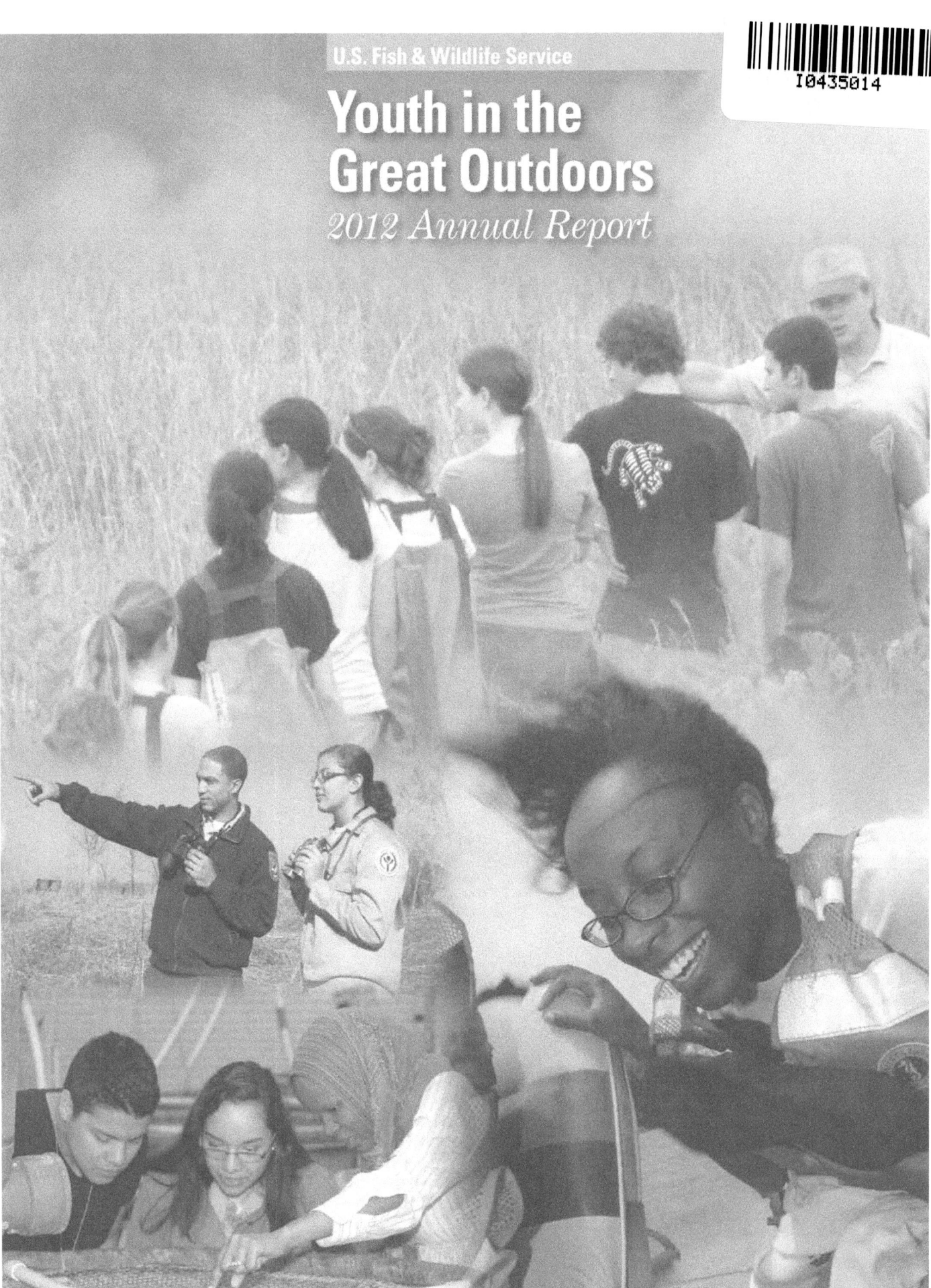

U.S. Fish & Wildlife Service

Youth in the Great Outdoors

2012 Annual Report

I0435014

Table of Contents

U.S. Fish and Wildlife Service Youth in the Great Outdoors
2012 Annual Report

Contributors

Region 1 (R1)
Bob Peyton, Dana Perez

Region 2 (R2)
Kenneth Garrahan, Gary Hutchison

Region 3 (R3)
Ann Marie Chapman, Maggie O'Connell

Region 4 (R4)
Sharon Fuller

Region 5 (R5)
Jennifer Lapis, Mao Lin, Sandy Perchetti,
Lamar Gore, Donald Freiday

Region 6 (R6)
Tina Dobrinsky, Diane (Dee) Emmons

Region 7 (R7)
Kristen Gilbert

Region 8 (R8)
Dara Rodriguez, Carol Damberg, Carolyn
Kolstad

Headquarters
National Wildlife Refuge System
Nathan Caldwell, Kevin Kilcullen,
Phil LePelch

Fisheries and Aquatic Conservation
Richard Christian, Denise Wagner

Migratory Bird Program
Alicia King, Rachel Levin

Endangered Species
Martha Balis Larsen, Lew Gorman

National Conservation Training Center
Drew Burnett, Steve Chase, Mary Danno,
Blaine Eckberg, Matt Gay, Juanita Gus-
tines, Nate Hawley, Georgia Jeppesen,
Dawn Lagrotteria, Chelsea McKinney,
Kathy Sholl, Jim Siegel, Kristin Simanek

Urban America Outdoors

U.S. Fish and Wildlife Service Director, Dan Ashe, participates in the Urban America Outdoors' seventh annual Urban Kids Fishing Derby in Kansas City.

"Building the next generation of conservation leaders to reflect the increasing diversity of our nation is a priority for the Fish and Wildlife Service. Our inclusive programs engage children while they are young, educate them as they grow, and offer exciting job opportunities when they are ready to enter the working world as young adults."
– Dan Ashe, Director
U.S. Fish and Wildlife Service

Executive Summary

The Youth in the Great Outdoors (YGO) initiative is a cornerstone of the U.S. Fish and Wildlife Service (Service) and is a critically important strategy for achieving the agency's mission over the long term. In fiscal year (FY) 2012 the Service continued its long tradition of providing programs that engage, educate, and employ millions of young people, their families, educators, and caregivers. The Service also made important advances in building our capacity to sustain this initiative over the long term. From the development of agency-wide employment reporting systems that will enable us to effectively track trends, to the publication of new policy chapters in the Service manual which establishes a framework for youth programming from the field to regional and headquarters (HQ) offices, the initiative is now poised for success in the 21st century. The purpose of this report is to highlight the work accomplished across the Service, at the field, regional and national office levels. Youth represent the future, and they are critical for the continued stewardship of the natural resources the Service conserves and protects. These highlights represent the tip of the iceberg of our agency's effort to build the next generation of conservation leaders who are committed and prepared to continue the Service's important work.

Introduction

Engaging, educating, and employing our nation's youth in conservation are major priorities for the Department of the Interior (Department), and in 2009 the YGO initiative was established.

The vision of YGO is to empower our employees and partners to develop the next generation of conservation and community leaders. The goals are to:
1) Engage youth from all backgrounds and geographic locations in the mission of the Service by providing them with opportunities to connect with and learn about plants, fish, wildlife, and their habitats;
2) Educate youth about natural resource conservation ethics/land stewardship; introduce them to the Service mission, lands, waters, wildlife, culture, and heritage; and challenge them to become involved in the management and conservation of natural and cultural resources; and
3) Employ youth to conserve, protect, and restore our environment. More information on the YGO initiative can be found at http://www.doi.gov/whatwedo/youth/index.cfm.

This report highlights the key activities underway in the Service in support of the YGO initiative. While the National Conservation Training Center (NCTC) and the National Wildlife Refuge System (NWRS) have the overall lead for YGO within the Service, this report will show that it is deeply integrated throughout all the national program areas, as well as regional and field units. And with NCTC's support for interagency coordination through the Department's Office of Youth, Partnerships, and Service (YPS), the Service is playing an important role in integrating the initiative across the Department. The Service reaches millions of youth, educators, and families with our programs each year. YGO presents us with an excellent opportunity to showcase our best efforts, which are critical to the vitality of the agency and the resources we conserve and protect. Key activities are organized in following areas: Employment; Education; Engagement; and Leadership, Coordination, and Training.

One of the top priorities of the YGO initiative is to increase the diversity of the youth that we engage, educate, and employ. Watch for highlights of diversity programs and activities in blue and green sidebars and text-boxes.

www.youthgo.gov

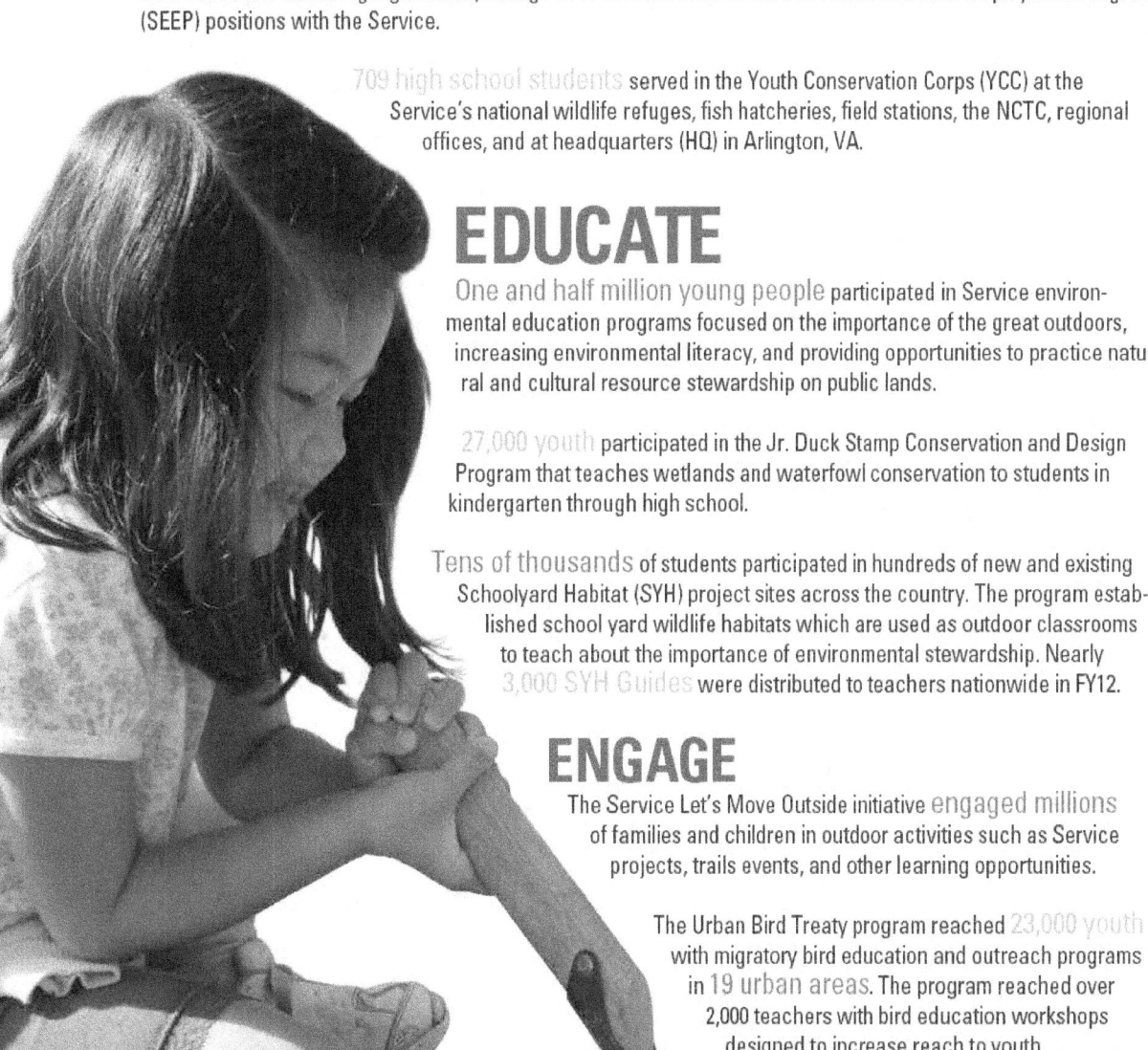

EMPLOY

During FY 2012 the Service employed 3,573 youth (ages 15 – 25) either directly or through partnerships with nonprofit organizations. This represents a 71% increase over the 2009 baseline, and is more than double the increase requested by the Department.

The Service worked with 18 additional nonprofit partnership organizations in FY 2012 for a total of 90 organizations to employ 1,325 youth who worked in all 50 states and 3 territories to help the Service achieve our resource management goals.

983 young people were employed in permanent and temporary positions.

556 students attending high school, college or vocational schools filled Student Education Employment Program (SEEP) positions with the Service.

709 high school students served in the Youth Conservation Corps (YCC) at the Service's national wildlife refuges, fish hatcheries, field stations, the NCTC, regional offices, and at headquarters (HQ) in Arlington, VA.

EDUCATE

One and half million young people participated in Service environmental education programs focused on the importance of the great outdoors, increasing environmental literacy, and providing opportunities to practice natural and cultural resource stewardship on public lands.

27,000 youth participated in the Jr. Duck Stamp Conservation and Design Program that teaches wetlands and waterfowl conservation to students in kindergarten through high school.

Tens of thousands of students participated in hundreds of new and existing Schoolyard Habitat (SYH) project sites across the country. The program established school yard wildlife habitats which are used as outdoor classrooms to teach about the importance of environmental stewardship. Nearly 3,000 SYH Guides were distributed to teachers nationwide in FY12.

ENGAGE

The Service Let's Move Outside initiative engaged millions of families and children in outdoor activities such as Service projects, trails events, and other learning opportunities.

The Urban Bird Treaty program reached 23,000 youth with migratory bird education and outreach programs in 19 urban areas. The program reached over 2,000 teachers with bird education workshops designed to increase reach to youth.

45 million people hunted, fished, observed or photographed wildlife at the Service's national wildlife refuges (NWR).

Employ

Using a variety of employment authorities and programs, and working with approximately 90 nonprofit partners, the Service is proud to announce the employment 3,573 youth ages 15 – 25, a 71% increase over our 2009 baseline year in which we employed a total of 2,084 youth. This is nearly double the goal set by the Department at the beginning of FY 2012. The following activities highlight key employment efforts.

Partnership Employment

Currently, nearly one-half of the youth who work on Service-related projects are employed by partners who work with our field stations, and regional and Washington offices on youth programs. Some of these relationships involve multiple organizations and funding sources that provide opportunities for youth that otherwise couldn't be supported. Our partners come in all shapes and sizes, from the large nationally known Student Conservation Association (SCA) and AmeriCorps, to our small locally based non-profit Refuge Friends' groups; from high schools to universities; and from state and local programs to tribal entities. The Service established 90 partnerships in all 50 states and employed over 1,325 youth. Please see the side bar for a list of our youth employment partners in FY 2012.

**U.S. Fish and Wildlife Service
Youth Employment Partner Organizations**

Alaska Science and Engineering Program
Alaska Sea Life Center
American Conservation Experience
AmeriCorps
Arctic Village Council
Arrupe Corporate Work Study Program
Audubon Society of NH
Ball State University
Black Swamp Bird Observatory
Bristol Bay Native Association
CA Conservation Corp
CA Waterfowl Association
Chesapeake Volunteers in Youth Services
Chickasaw Youth Program
City of Columbia Missouri
City of Salmon
College of Southern Idaho
Conservation Corps Iowa
Conservation Corps Minnesota & Iowa
Ding Darling Wildlife Society
Easter Seals of Southern GA, Inc.
Environment for the Americas
Fairbanks Soil and Water
 Conservation District
Franklin College
Friends of Alaska National Wildlife Refuges
Friends of Deer Flat
Friends of Great Swamp NWR
Friends of Nisqually NWR
Friends of Northwest Hatcheries
Friends of Southern Oregon
Friends of Tampa Bay
Friends of the Rydell Refuge Association
Friends of Wichita Mountain
Friends of Willamette Valley
Georgia Southern University
Great Basin Bird Observatory
Greening of Detroit
Groundwork Denver
Humboldt County Office of Education
Indiana University
Indiana University - Bloomington
Job Corps
Klamath Outdoor Science School
KUPU, Hawaii Youth Conservation Corps
Kuskowim Native Association
Manomet Center for Conservation Science

Mile High Youth Corps
Montana Conservation Corps
Mussett Family Foundation, Inc.
National Audubon Society
National Park Service
Native Village of Eyak
Nez Perce Tribe
Northwest Youth Corps
Northwoods Stewardship Center
Ogalalla Commons
OR Watershed Enhancement Board
Orutsararmuit Native Council
Otis Bay Inc.
Ottawa Soil & Water Conservation District
Penn State University Coop Unit
Portland State University
Purdue University
Quinault Indian Nation
Refuge Friends Inc.
Saint Michaels College
Sanibel Captiva Island Foundation
Seney Natural History Association
Smith Valley/Mason Valley Conservation
 Districts, NV
Southwest Minnesota Private Industry Council
St. Joseph the Worker Corp
Student Conservation Association
Tanana Chiefs Conference
The Nature Conservancy
Tishomingo Schools
Tok Chamber of Commerce
Trout Unlimited
Tuscon Youth Development
University of Alaska Fairbanks/Wildlife
 Conservation Society Arctic Program
University of Alaska Southeast
University of FL
University of Hi UHHIP PIPES Program
University of Maine, Sparrow Research
University of Maryland
University of Montana
Vermont Youth Conservation Corps
Walker River Paiute Tribe
Washington Conservation Corps
Wells National Estuarine Research Reserve
Wetland Conservation
Wisconsin Department of Natural Resources

R1 / Oregon Coast National Wildlife Refuge, Oregon
HQ / National Conservation Training Center, West Virginia

NCTC provided funding for Celebra las Playeras Latino Youth Internship Program, an innovative Environment for the Americas (EFTA) program, which supported four bilingual Hispanic American college students and recent graduates as paid environmental education interns on NWRs in California, Oregon and Colorado. The interns engaged directly with growing, yet underserved, Latino communities near their refuge, educating them about migratory birds and wetland conservation. Outreach at the Oregon Coast NWR focused on the function of marine and coastal environments with particular emphasis on its wildlife. Intern Sammy Chavez successfully led two interpretive paddle trips for other young Latinos in the community, translated refuge brochures into Spanish, and engaged over 2,000 general visitors (including some Spanish speakers) in informal interpretive talks about Oregon's marine life such as the peregrine falcon, black oystercatcher, common murre, sea stars, and more.

Hawaii's college students teaching aquatic resource management techniques to high school students.

You don't need to be bilingual to know these youths are having fun. (Oregon Coast NWR)

R1 / Pacific Islands Fish and Wildlife Office (PIFWO), Hawaii

Native Hawaiian students are underserved and underrepresented in the conservation field. The PIFWO entered into partnerships with Oahu Refuges, the Department of Defense, Hawaii State's Division of Aquatic Resources, and private land owners to allow for restoration of aquatic habitat for candidate and rare species. These partnerships employed and mentored college students during the summer through conservation focused projects where they acquired experience and skills in monitoring, capturing and marking rare species. These students then taught these skills to other predominantly native Hawaiian high school students, who in turn conducted learning stations for visitors at the Kalaeloa unit of the Pearl Harbor NWR. The students gave a presentation on protecting and conserving native aquatic species to over 100 college freshmen. These mentoring projects provided students with useable, marketable skills, which will plant the seeds for conservation careers in Hawaii.

R3 / Midwest Regional Office, Minnesota

For the first time, the Midwest Regional Office's Refuges program hosted two immigrant students from Kenya, who are attending college in the Twin Cities area. Iman Mohamed and Hafsa Hussein were recruited with assistance from Service partner STEP-UP Achieve. This City of Minneapolis program connects businesses with the next generation of talented and diverse workers, provides critical hands-on job skills for young people, and builds a stronger Twin Cities workforce. Iman worked in the Division of Realty and Hafsa worked in the Division of Budget and Facilities. In addition to performing clerical duties at the regional office throughout the summer, both enrollees teamed up with the YCC crew at Minnesota Valley NWR to participate in environmental education activities. Iman was especially excited about his first experience fishing on the refuge.

YCC enrollees Iman Mohamed (left) and Hafsa Hussein (right) enjoy a day out of the office at Minnesota Valley NWR.

R4 / Alabama Field Office, Alabama

This summer, Spanish Fort High School senior Katie Dankovic spent eight weeks with the Service's Alabama Field Office as a scholar in the 2012 Hutton Junior Fisheries Biology Program. The Hutton Program was created by the American Fisheries Society in an effort to attract females, minorities and members of underrepresented communities interested in fisheries science careers. Fifteen students were chosen out of 79 applicants, and biologists from the Alabama Field Office were selected as Katie's mentors. Service biologists took Katie under their wings, and helped her gain hands-on experience in science. Katie participated in a variety of activities, including mussel surveys, necropsies, and the removal of invasive island apple snails. This fall, Katie entered the University of South Alabama as a freshman, where she is majoring in marine biology.

The interns and volunteers planting at demonstration parcel in the Laguna Cartagena National Wildlife Refuge in the lower watershed. Photo: USFWS.

R4 and R1 / Refuges

In 2012, the Service's Southeast and Pacific Regions partnered with the U.S. Coral Reef Task Force to employ four student interns as part of the Governor Tauese P.F. Sunia Coral Reef Conservation Summer Internship Program. These interns gained first-hand experience working on habitat restoration efforts on national wildlife refuge lands, farms, and other private lands. Two interns worked in Puerto Rico and two in Hawaii. The Sunia Internship recognizes the late Governor of American Samoa for his outstanding leadership and contributions to the conservation of coral reef ecosystems and provides students with career-enhancing experience in coral reef conservation and management initiatives in the Caribbean and Pacific jurisdictions. The internship program is a collaboration of many partners including the Department's Office of Insular Affairs, U.S. Department of Agriculture-Natural Resources Conservation Service, the National Oceanic Atmospheric Administration, the Conservation Trust of Puerto Rico, and the Service.

Career Discovery Internship Program
R7 / Alaska Regional Office, Alaska
R5 / Northeast Regional Office, Massachusetts
R4 / Southeast Regional Office, Georgia
R3/ Midwest Regional Office, Minnesota

The Service's Career Discovery Internship Program (CDIP) received The Wildlife Society 2012 Diversity Award which recognizes outstanding efforts in promoting ethnic and gender diversity in the natural resource professions, especially wildlife conservation and education. The program, which originated in the Northeast Region, has grown from 20 students in 2008 to over 50 students in 2012, representing states across four Service Regions. Approximately 193 students participated at more than 70 Service field offices across the regions since the program began. CDIP was designed as an emersion experience for students and staff, and represents just one of the successful partnerships the Service has established with the Student Conservation Association (SCA), which plays a critical role in recruiting and planning logistics. Students gain hands-on conservation skills, form bonds with Service mentors, and achieve personal, intellectual and physical goals. The program also provides staff the opportunity to engage culturally and ethnically diverse youth at Service field stations. CDIP job positions range from visitor services, facilities management, maintenance, biological, and public affairs. Interns attended a week long training session at the beginning of the summer before heading to individual field stations for the eight week long internship.

R6 / Chase Lake National Wildlife Refuge, North Dakota

Two crews from the Conservation Corps Minnesota and Iowa came to Chase Lake NWR in 2012 to help with invasive species removal and wildlife monitoring projects. One crew focused most of their time on invasive species removal and the other participated in pelican banding. The crew helped carry the pelicans to the banding stations, placed bands on the birds, and recorded band data. Each crew had many educational opportunities as well, including hearing presentations on topics such as national wildlife refuges, a native bee pollen study, and invasive species identification and management. With all these unique experiences, the Conservation Corps crew learned important environmental conservation concepts while enjoying the rolling prairie!

R7 / Alaska Regional Office

The Alaska Region partners with eight tribal groups to actively stem the disconnection between young tribal members and the natural environment. Activities begin in elementary school, and in some cases, the students end up becoming conservation professionals. Alissa Nadine Joseph for example is a native of Bethel Alaska, a small hub village (only accessible by boat or plane) for over 25,000 people that live in the Yukon/Kuskowim Delta of Alaska, where her family practices a traditional subsistence lifestyle. For the past several summers, Alissa has interned through the Orutsaramiut Native Council and the Service's Partners for Fisheries Management Program working on various fisheries resource monitoring projects. Now a biology major at the University of Alaska Fairbanks, she was hired by the Alaska Department of Fish and Game as part of the Board Support Section for the regulatory process for fisheries. Alissa's story is happening all over Alaska as the Service and tribal partners continue to spark elementary students' interest in conservation and nurture their interests through high school and college.

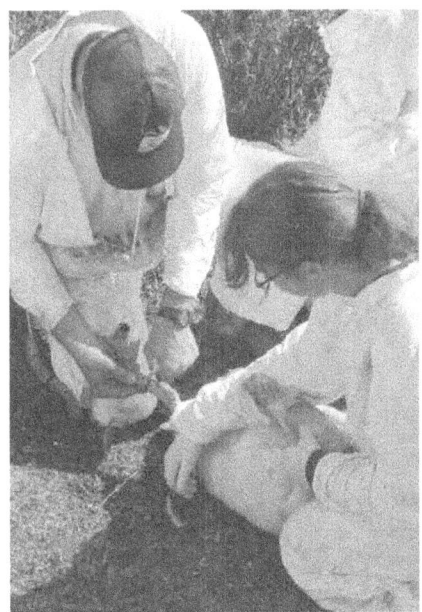

Corps member helping with pelican banding project.

Alissa Nadine Joseph, an intern with the Service's Office of Subsistence Management has developed important conservation skills in her hometown of Bethel.

Alaska Native students participate in real-life science to spark and interest in conservation.

Alaska Maritime NWR support the science instruction at the Camp Quagan Tayagungin culture camp in UnAlaska, Alaska.

HQ / National Wildlife Refuge System, Virginia

This is the second year HQ funded student internships through the Tribal College Internship Program. This program reaches out to under-represented students enrolled in tribal colleges through a partnership with the Student Conservation Association. Intern Dominick Harris is a native Alaskan from the Aleut Tribe who currently attends the North Seattle Community College. He worked as a biology intern on the 25,000 acre National Elk Refuge and spent most of his summer inventorying and mapping vegetation. Harris also worked on various other projects such as noxious weed eradication, collecting scat for a climatology study, counting bison and monitoring their movement onto and off the refuge, conducting forage sampling surveys with the staff biologist, and entering historic elk collar data from the 1970s and 80s to aid in assessing elk migration trends.

Refuge biologist Eric Cole, right, received help from Dominick Harris during his forage sampling work.

HQ / National Wildlife Refuge System, Virginia

The 2012 Trails Inventory Program was the conclusion of a nationwide effort begun in 2011 to compile a comprehensive and accurate database for all trails and trail assets within the Service. This partnership with the SCA provided an amazing opportunity for 16 young adults to grow as conservation leaders. The 2012 program completed the overall survey in four months with six interns, "ground truthing" previously un-surveyed trails in the refuges. By documenting the footprint of trails as well as their associated features and deficiencies, the SCA provided the Service and Federal Highways Administration with a full account of the values and conditions of their trail systems. Using this completed database, the Service can make more educated assessments and plans for repair and management of our trail systems in the future. Combining the technical experience working with GPS/GIS and the personal growth found through living and working with new people in new places, this program provided a powerful experience for the interns.

Student Education Employment Program

The Service's SEEP employed 556 students attending high school, college or vocational schools in FY 2012. The two components of SEEP are the Student Temporary Employment Program (STEP), and the Student Career Experience Program (SCEP). The SEEP was replaced with the new Pathways Program in FY 2012, which provides students in high schools, colleges, trade schools and other qualifying educational institutions with paid opportunities to work in federal agencies and explore careers while completing their education. For more information on the new Pathways Program, see www.opm.gov/hiringreform/pathways/.

R1 / Sheldon - Hart Mountain National Wildlife Refuge Complex, Nevada and Oregon

Sheldon – Hart Mountain NWR Complex employed two STEP employees as firefighters for wildland fire suppression on and off refuge lands. They also helped in national suppression duties, including assignments in Arizona and around Oregon, and various refuge fuels projects such as juniper thinning, layout of new units, and prescribed fire. When not working on normal fire projects or suppression, the staff assisted the two refuges with routine maintenance, fence removal, posting restrictions, painting kiosks, and the horse round up.

R2 /Southwest Region Division of Diversity and Civil Rights Office, New Mexico

The Southwest Region is proud to support the Wounded Warrior Project by participating in Operation Warfighter – an effort to help wounded veterans gain new skills that will help them reenter the workforce. The Division of Diversity and Civil Rights Office participated in Warriors to Work recruitment venues and to date, has hired four wounded warriors – two in Oklahoma, one in Arizona, and one in South Texas. The Service looks forward to increasing involvement in this worthy effort. To learn more about the Wounded Warrior Project, see http://www.fws.gov/southwest/AboutUs/vets.html.

R3 / Minnesota Valley National Wildlife Refuge, Minnesota

Through an on-going relationship with the University of Wisconsin-Stevens Point's College of Natural Resources, the Midwest Region hired STEP student Brittany Ruttenberg as a biological science technician at Minnesota Valley NWR. Brittany is a junior majoring in both biology and wildlife ecology. She is also President of the Stevens Point chapter of Minorities in Agriculture, Natural Resources and Related Sciences (MANRRS). According to supervisor Vicki Sherry, Brittany "is a very outgoing, academically strong, diverse candidate who has been a leader in the MANRRS program at Steven's Point. She does not have a lot of field experience yet and she could benefit from a field experience with the Service." At Minnesota Valley, Brittany's responsibilities included invasive species control, water management, plant and animal surveys and GIS mapping. Following her experience, Brittany plans to pursue a Pathways Program opportunity. She said, "Working with the U.S. Fish and Wildlife Service this summer has been an incredibly valuable experience. I feel like I'm learning something new every day!"

STEP employee Brittany Ruttenberg uses a GPS unit to map invasive plant species populations on Minnesota Valley NWR.

R5 / John Heinz National Wildlife Refuge, Pennsylvania

Tajuan Levy's story is a perfect example of the opportunities the Service provides for young people looking for a pathway to conservation careers and leadership. First hired into the Conservation Internship Program in 2009, Tajuan wanted to do something "different" during his summer break. He worked as a visitor services intern at Moosehorn NWR in Maine, learning about the NWRS and what it meant to be part of the Service family. Subsequently Tajuan looked for another summer job with the Service in facilities maintenance, utilizing the engineering technology skills he was learning at school. Tajuan's next step with the Service was applying for, and accepting, a SCEP position at the John Heinz NWR as a Facilities Operation Specialist. Tajuan's superior work ethic, dedication and willingness to learn will pay off when he is converted to a permanent Service employee after graduation.

Tajuan Levy at John Heinz NWR

R7 / Arctic National Wildlife Refuge, Alaska

Alfredo Soto, a zoology student from Southern Illinois University, emerged from the warm aircraft into the freezing temperatures and 40 MPH winds typical of the arctic coast in early June. Joining the rest of the crew, he set to the task of hauling gear off the lake to establish the camp that he called home for the next six weeks. Several months earlier, Alfredo was hired as a SCEP employee at the Arctic NWR, where he studied imperiled shorebird populations as part of an international effort to conserve declining species. He worked alongside experienced ornithologists and became skilled at shorebird identification, banding, and sample collection. He looks forward to returning to Alaska next summer to join another research expedition, and he plans to attend graduate school beginning in fall 2013.

Alfredo Soto examines a lemming on the coastal plain of the Arctic NWR.

R8 / Klamath Falls Fish and Wildlife Office, Oregon

Davis Hernandez, an environmental science student at the Oregon Institute of Technology, became a SCEP employee in the Klamath Falls Fish and Wildlife Office in March 2012. Davis is interested in various aspects of wildlife, regularly volunteers at Badger Run Wildlife Rehab, knows basic taxidermy techniques, and has experience in graphics design. Davis has tribal heritage through the Yaqui people. He assisted with activities related to the Service Partners for Fish and Wildlife program and the Connecting People with Nature (CPWN) priority. His work responsibilities included: project monitoring, assisting in site surveys, preparation of reports, assisting in local community projects that educate youth, and providing technical assistance on raptor-related issues. He developed his senior project on golden eagle monitoring in Oregon. Davis provides a valuable addition to the Klamath Falls staff with his high level of enthusiasm for his work.

SCEP Student, Davis Hernandez (Center), planting native plants at OIT Schoolyard Habitat Project.

Youth Conservation Corps

A total of 709 high school students served in the Youth Conservation Corps (YCC) at the Service's national wildlife refuges, fish hatcheries, field stations, the NCTC, regional offices, and at HQ in Arlington, VA. These summer jobs are available to students ages 15-18, and for many, it is the first paying job they've ever had. The students are typically recruited in local communities through newspaper announcements, high school job fairs, science classes and clubs, and state labor offices, or during special visits to the schools by Service staff.

R2 / Sevilleta National Wildlife Refuge, New Mexico

The 2012 YCC crew has a lot to be proud of after this summer. The crew was comprised of two high school students from Socorro, and two from Belen. They worked hard each day, while maintaining great attitudes and an open mind toward the tasks ahead. No matter how hard they were working, the crew always kept an ear out for a possible environmental lesson to be learned. One crew member commented, "Together we learned the importance of preserving our environment and maintaining the habitats the refuge works so hard to protect. We discovered a sense of ownership and responsibility for the world around us, and how even with minimal effort we can have a positive impact on all of it."

YCC crew member Colten Wheeler works happily and persistently, tightening a metal brace together right before concrete is poured to secure the brace in place.

R3 / Detroit River National Wildlife Refuge, Michigan

The Detroit River International Wildlife Refuge YCC crew spent most of their summer planting 150 sapling oaks. Throughout the summer, the crew continually visited and cared for their nascent oak trees to encourage their survival. One day, the crew had the rare privilege of a visit from Congressman John Dingell and his staff who brought lunch for everyone. YCC enrollee Courtney Cunningham reflected, "Coming from the city I never thought I would be doing the work I did every day for eight weeks. What was really cool was the feeling of getting something done for a cause. Not only were we helping ourselves, we were helping our children and our children's children. This new experience is something that I will remember and cherish for the rest of my life. I've met so many new people and made so many good friends. This is one of the experiences I will remember forever."

R4 / Cabo Rojo and Laguna Cartegena National Wildlife Refuges, Puerto Rico

Twelve students participated in the 2012 YCC program working with different projects such as maintaining a wildlife observation tower and refuge trail, which included sanding and painting of the structures. However, favorite activities included working at the visitor center, the greenhouse, and the reforestation of refuge areas. One of the YCC crew members coined a wonderful phrase while planting at Cabo Rojo NWR, "Sembrar vida es sembrar alegría" which means planting life is planting happiness.

Crew members plant a tree from the nursery.

Crew members care for saplings in the nursery.

NCTC YCC crew assist with trail work at Canaan Valley National Wildlife Refuge

R4 / Orangeburg National Fish Hatchery, South Carolina
HQ / National Conservation Training Center, West Virginia

In cooperation with the NCTC, Orangeburg National Fish Hatchery developed and implemented a YCC program. The crew of six accomplished a variety of tasks over the summer, from preparing cane poles and staffing booths for the hatchery's annual Kids Fishing Day, to learning about fish species, habitats, and the role of fish hatcheries and the Fisheries Program while caring for the fish ponds. Students also talked with hatchery staff about careers and how their summer job experience could be a catalyst for a career in the Service. The experience allowed the students to take on leadership roles by teaching others, grasp fundamental conservation concepts, and become more comfortable with public speaking.

R5 / Rachel Carson National Wildlife Refuge, Maine

On the 50th anniversary year of the publication of Rachel Carson's book "A Silent Spring," the Rachel Carson NWR in Maine hosted its 12th YCC crew. The five person crew and crew leader accomplished a great deal of work on the refuge, and had fun learning important wildlife and natural resource-related lessons. Finished projects included building a deck, installing wayside signs, invasive species removal and piping plover work. The crew also took a field trip to the University of New England's Marine Rehabilitation Center for an educational tour. Feedback from the crew was extremely positive with most of them commenting on how they would apply to do it again next year and would recommend the summer job to a friend.

R6 / Creston National Fish Hatchery, Montana

This was the third year of the Northwest Montana Native YCC, managed from Creston National Fish Hatchery in Kalispell, Montana. The number of applicants more than doubled from the previous two years with almost 60 applicants for the 15 positions. The crew spent six of the eight weeks performing conservation work on the Flathead Reservation. This year the crew also had the opportunity to work for two weeks installing the Creston Nature Explore outdoor classroom (see page 27 for more on the Nature Explore program).

"Tidepooling" environmental education event with interns and YCC crew members on the rocky coasts of Maine.

R7 / Kenai National Wildlife Refuge, Alaska

The YCC program at Kenai NWR has a long and successful history of engaging young adults in conservation and resource management with an emphasis on diverse and challenging projects and a dynamic environmental education program. During the eight week program, this season's projects introduced YCC enrollees to historic cabin restoration and the history of European settlement on the Kenai Peninsula; riparian habitat protection; portage trail maintenance and paddling in the remote Wilderness of the Swan Lake Canoe System; trail construction and maintenance; Leave No Trace ethics; wildfire ecology and management; and bear awareness.

For some enrollees this was their first job, for others it was their first experience swinging a tool or camping on the refuge, but for all it was an exciting opportunity to work and learn outdoors with a tightly knit group of peers. For more information on the YCC program at Kenai NWR see www.fws.gov/refuge/Kenai/community/2012_article/07132012.html

On Alaska Maritime National Wildlife Refuge YCC spearheaded a creative float that won first prize at annual community parade.

After the marine debris clean up, enrollee Anelise Zimmer reflects, "One of my favorite moments was the feeling after you clean a bunch of marine debris and you see the huge stack and you see how clean the beach is...and you feel like you made a difference."

Kodiak YCC enrollees looking down on the town of Kodiak, Alaska.

San Luis NWRC YCC crew working with refuge staff to construct a split-rail fence at a new nature trailhead parking area at the Merced NWR. - Photo Credit: FWS

R8 / San Luis National Wildlife Refuge, California

The San Luis NWR Complex in Los Banos, California has been sponsoring YCC crews annually since 2006. Ranging in size from 6 to 14 members, this year's crew employed 12 young people from the local community to complete tasks in support of the development and maintenance of the refuge's wildlife and habitat resources. The crew's work teaches its members the need and responsibility of maintaining and managing those resources for future generations of Americans – and can spark an interest in a career in wildlife conservation as well. In addition to performing vital work contributing to wildlife and habitat conservation, this year's crew developed self-discipline and work ethics, learned how to relate to supervisors and peers, and built lasting bonds with youth from other backgrounds.

HQ / National Conservation Training Center, West Virginia

The work-learn-earn program employed seven students full-time for eight weeks at NCTC, where the youth performed important outdoor and indoor work while gaining knowledge and experience about the Service, ecology and conservation careers. The youth developed work skills while building and improving hiking trails, tending native plants, maintaining boundary lines, removing invasive plants, and caring for young trees in reforestation sites. The youth also went offsite to perform service projects and take educational tours of other federal agency sites including Antietam National Battlefield, the Leetown Fish Hatchery, and Canaan Valley NWR.

Educate

The Service has been building environmental literacy through education for decades. Our regional and field staff educates and engages millions of young people, educators, and families through outdoor experiences based on local needs and realities. While no two environmental education programs are exactly alike, many can be grouped into programs that have similar characteristics in the methodologies used and audiences targeted. Volunteers are critically important in environmental education and they enable the Service to reach many thousands more people. The following highlights provide a snapshot of the most current and effective programs for building environmental literacy and engaging the nation's young people in the important business of conservation.

Partnership Programs

Refuge Explorers
R1 / Willapa National Wildlife Refuge, Washington

The fourth grade students of Pacific County, Washington studied the soils, plants and animals of the Willapa NWR to become "Refuge Explorers" as part of the on-going environmental education partnership program with the Friends of Willapa NWR. Twenty-two volunteers taught hands-on lessons in which over 200 students from six schools learned about the refuge system, adaptations, food webs, science and habitat restoration. Students sharpened observation skills, kept a nature journal, and used critical thinking to craft inferences about refuge wildlife. Students tested their inferences on an excursion to the refuge and reported their findings to refuge staff. FY 2012 program highlights included dip netting in the bay for marine species, the discovery of an elk's leg bone along a trail, and finding bear tracks. For more information, including a video, see: www.fws.gov/willapa/education/education.html

Leadership in Nature
R2 / Santa Ana and Laguna Atascosa National Wildlife Refuges, Texas

The Santa Ana and Laguna Atascosa NWRs partnered with the Edinburg Scenic Wetlands and World Birding Center to conduct a week-long camp for high school students, entitled "Leadership in Nature." Six high school students from across the Rio Grande Valley spent the week learning about conservation issues and careers. Some of the activities the students enjoyed were bird banding, a tram tour at Santa Ana, talks by the South Texas Refuge Complex Law Enforcement and Fire Crews, and kayaking and camping at Laguna Atascosa. Refuge managers from Santa Ana and Lower Rio Grande Valley attended a mentor lunch, where they discussed their personal career paths and helped to guide the students in their future endeavors. The "Leadership in Nature" students also spent a day with the refuge YCC interns. Each group shared their experiences in hopes that the YCC interns will consider the "Leadership in Nature" program next year and vice versa. The week ended with a camp out at Laguna Atascosa, where the students practiced their night photography skills.

In the snow fort lab, Blair Community Schools' students measure mass of snow pack and calculate density.

Blair Community Schools Outdoor Education Partnership
R3 / DeSoto National Wildlife Refuge, Iowa

Imagine a classroom without walls and science, math, social studies, and language arts lessons all focused on natural phenological events like the fall migration. This is the reality for the students from Blair Community Schools, who have been using the DeSoto NWR as their outdoor classroom for the past seven years. The experience is not only making school fun, but helps to improve student achievement in science. Last school year (2011-2012), the 5th, 8th and 11th grades completed baseline testing for state science standards. Blair's science scores were above the state average in each of the three grade levels tested. "This is a first time snapshot," said Mark Gutschow, Blair assistant principal and the school partnership coordinator. "It is encouraging to be above the state average. District scores are higher than the state average for a variety of reasons, however, in my opinion, the partnership with DeSoto has directly contributed to higher student achievement."

Blair Community Schools and DeSoto NWR partnership logo.

Family Nature Club
R4 / Wolf Creek National Fish Hatchery, Kentucky

In partnership with the Russell County Public Libraries, Wolf Creek NFH implemented the year-round Family Nature Club after school to offer families time to be actively engaged in hands-on activities while learning about nature. The club's primary goals are to promote sound conservation practices and to educate others about nature and the environment. Monthly meetings include educational programs on various topics such as leaf printing, dissecting owl pellets, nature scavenger hunts, night hikes, fishing, outdoor survival tips, and interacting with live animals. Meetings rotate between the library and fish hatchery. For more information on the program see www.fws.gov/wolfcreek/

Lacey, New Jersey Township High School Advanced Placement Environmental Education
R5 / E. B. Forsythe National Wildlife Refuge, New Jersey

Forsythe NWR partnered with the Lacey, New Jersey Township High School Advanced Placement Environmental Education class to develop hands-on learning activities in support of the school's curriculum and the students' experiential learning options. With the refuge serving as an outdoor classroom, students use plant and animal indicator species to study the process of eutrophication while conducting a chemical

analysis of the waters of Gull Pond. The tests included pH, DO, nitrates, phosphates, clarity and temperature, all of which are involved in the eutrophication process and affect population numbers and types of species present at the time of the study. The students took their data back to class to discuss their findings together and to form conclusions for the study. Part of this project was funded through the NCTC Regional Funding Initiative (RFI). See page 41 for more information on the RFI.

Kids C.A.N. (Care about Nature)
R6 / Great Plains Nature Center, Kansas

Kids C.A.N. (Care about Nature) Day, sponsored by the Wichita Downtown Kiwanis Club, is held annually at the Great Plains Nature Center. The center is a partnership among the Service, the Kansas Department of Wildlife, Parks and Tourism, and the City of Wichita. Fifth grade students participate in nature-related activities focusing on water, soil/earth, plants, animals, and conservation. The activities meet many state education outcomes and are designed to encourage students to appreciate the natural world and become better stewards of its resources. The predominately hands-on outdoor event gives the students an opportunity to be up close and personal with the natural world. Approximately 250 students from 12-15 schools attended the three-day event.

BioBlitz
R8 / San Francisco Bay National Wildlife Refuge, California

Nearly 200 people including many youth arrived at the Don Edwards-San Francisco Bay NWR over a 24-hour period to become field scientists, documenting every living organism that crossed their path as part of the December 10, 2011 BioBlitz event. From 2 p.m. December 10 to 2 p.m. December 11, scientists, educators, and members of the community logged 215 species in a targeted area of the refuge. In addition to the plant, avian, mammalian, and fish species that were observed and confirmed, there was also phytoplankton, insects, and one mollusk. Participants were given data sheets to record all the species they observed, and were encouraged to enter the data directly onto the website, or submit their data sheets to refuge staff to receive credit for the final report. The refuge partnered on the event with other federal agencies, municipal government, and multiple non-profit organizations and universities. A final report and the individually-logged observations can be found on the refuge's website at www.fws.gov/desfbay. More information available from www.fws.gov/FieldNotes/regmap.cfm?arskey=31241&callingKey=region&callingValue=8

Liming Chao attempts to look through the spotting scope during a bird walk while her mother Sunny, and sister Ping-Ya looks on. - Photo Credit: Alex Baranda

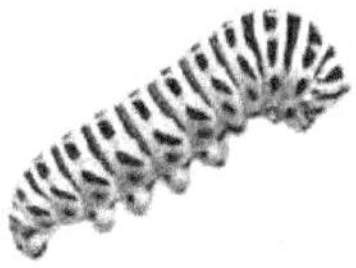

Wildlife Forever Partnership
HQ / Fish and Aquatic Conservation Program

HQ Fisheries staff partnered with Wildlife Forever (WF) to present the first-ever "Fish Make You Smarter" Awards for the best essays in WF's State Fish Art Contest. This is a highly successful nationwide conservation education program combining art and science which catches the imagination of students, fosters discovery of the natural world, and increases awareness of and respect for aquatic resources. Along with their artwork, students submitted essays from throughout the United States. Winning essays along with art will be featured in the 2013 education issue of "Eddies" magazine. For more information on the contest see www.wildlifeforever.org/contest. To read the winning essays in Eddies, see www.fws.gov/eddies/.

Arthur Carhart National Wilderness Training Center Education Program
HQ / National Conservation Training Center, West Virginia

In partnership with the U.S. Forest Service and the National Park Service, NCTC provides critically important staff support for the education specialist position at the Arthur Carhart National Wilderness Training Center in Montana. The training center's mission is to preserve the values and benefits of wilderness for present and future generations by connecting agency employees and the public with their wilderness heritage through training, information, and education. Key accomplishments of the center's education program include:

- *Wilderness Investigation*
  A new interagency wilderness education training and curriculum project, *Wilderness Investigations (WI)*, provides a standards-correlated and place-based toolkit, live teacher training workshops, printed and downloadable teaching materials, online investigation-specific training, and a WI teacher networking site for sharing, problem-solving, and program

announcements. WI topics are focused on key elements of the Wilderness Act of 1964 and include classroom, field, and family components. Every WI investigation includes project-based/hands-on activities, and many lead to service learning opportunities. In FY 2012 there were 17 workshops reaching 256 teachers in 5 western states. www.carhart.wilderness.net

- *Outdoor Explorer Mentoring Program*
  The program was launched in Missoula in 2011 as a partnership among a federal agency, a non-profit that serves underserved youth, and a non-profit organization that includes college-age youth focused on outdoor activities. The agency partner acts as advisor and main funding agent. The non-profit serving underserved youth markets monthly activities to their clients, helps plan activities, and bills the agency partner for expenses. The college-age youth are trained as mentors, plan activities with program partners and lead monthly activities for underserved youth. In FY 2012 the program was expanded to Helena and Bozeman reaching 327 mentors, and 470 underserved youth. www.carhart.wilderness.net

Student Climate and Conservation Congress (SC3)
HQ / National Conservation Training Center, West Virginia

The Student Climate and Conservation Congress (SC3), held at NCTC each summer since 2009, was developed in partnership with the Green Schools Alliance for 100 highly dedicated high school student environmental activists. During SC3 the students interacted with Department and global environmental leaders to build their own leadership capabilities, gain the knowledge, skills and tools to address natural resource challenges and better serve their schools and home communities. Participants leave the event with action plans for engaging their own communities in conservation. www.greenschoolsalliance.org/students/student-climate-conservation-congress-sc3

Natural Resource Conservation Education Award
HQ / National Conservation Training Center, West Virginia

Each year, NCTC partners with the USDA 4-H Program to present the Natural Resource Conservation Education Award at the North American Wildlife and Natural Resources Conference. This year's project, the Geographic Information Systems Mapping Replication and Expansion Project, brings young Americans into the outdoors and meets local

California 4-H delegation and Service employee Debbie Good prepare to use GPS post and cable infrastructure.

needs at NWRs and/or National Fish Hatcheries in a unique way through the use of mapping technology. 4-H students in four different states mapped trails, habitat management projects, interpretive signs, and even utilized Google Earth to showcase special sites that may be of interest to visitors.

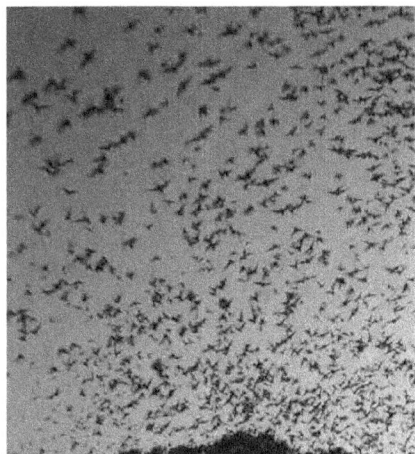

BatsLIVE
HQ / National Conservation Training Center, West Virginia
NCTC's Division of Education Outreach (DEO) partnered with a number of federal agencies, including the U.S. Forest Service, and the Prince William Network to develop BatsLIVE, a distance learning program dedicated to educating youth around the world about the value of bats and the threatening issues they face. A three-part webcast was developed to teach students the importance of bat and habitat conservation, demonstrate how to build a bat house, and answer questions. The first webcast was broadcast from Bracken Caves near San Antonio, TX with approximately 46,000 viewers. The series ended with a webinar called "Caves and Karst: The World Beneath Our Feet." To learn more about the program, view the webcasts, or to learn how you can become involved please see www.batslive.pwnet.org/

Inspiring Ocean Stewardship through Art, Photography and Film
HQ / National Conservation Training Center, West Virginia
NCTC, in partnership with the Department of the Interior's Senior Ocean Policy Team, supported Coastal America Foundation's "Inspiring Ocean Stewardship through Art, Photography and Film," coordinated by Coastal America's Coastal Ecosystem Learning Centers.

Over 1,500 entries from 20 Centers were narrowed down to eight national winners. The eight winning students and their chaperones were brought to Washington, DC to participate in events around Capitol Hill Ocean Week (June 5-8, 2012) and World Oceans Day (June 8, 2012). The students received recognition and attended sponsored events held by Coastal America Foundation and its partners including: National Geographic Society, Commission for Environmental Cooperation's North American Protected Area Network, National Marine Sanctuary Foundation, and the Smithsonian Institution.

Agency Programs

Jr. Duck Stamp
HQ / Migratory Birds
The Federal Junior Duck Stamp Conservation and Design Program (JDS) is a dynamic arts curriculum that teaches wetlands and waterfowl conservation to students in kindergarten through high school. The program incorporates scientific and wildlife management principles into a visual arts curriculum, with participants completing a JDS design as their visual "term papers." Sales of Jr. Duck Stamps generated more than $55,000 for the program, which reached more than 27,000 youth in all 50 states and Washington, DC in FY 2012. www.fws.gov/juniorduck/. Highlights from this year's program include:

2012 Best of Show, pair of Hooded Mergansers

Art contest entries

■ *California Junior Duck Stamp Program*
R8 / Sacramento National Wildlife Refuge Complex
Artwork from over 3,500 school-aged waterfowl artists throughout the state was judged during the 22nd Annual California Federal Junior Duck Stamp Contest in Chico. The California Federal Junior Duck Stamp Program is coordinated by Marilyn Gamette, and facilitated by the Service's Sacramento NWR Complex. Partnerships included California Waterfowl, Central Valley Joint Venture, the California Rice Commission, California Department of Water Resources, and other

Judges with 2012 Best of Show winner

federal, state, private, and non-profit environmental conservation and education agencies. A panel of 10 judges was tasked with selecting 100 winners. In addition to the art, three conservation messages were selected from each age group to receive awards. These messages were submitted on the artwork entry form and judged for originality, understanding of wetland and waterfowl conservation, and inspiration. All 100 winning artwork entries and 12 winning conservation messages will be on display throughout the year at various California events. More information available at www.fws.gov/FieldNotes/regmap.cfm?arskey=31680&callingKey=region&callingValue=8

Schoolyard Habitat/Outdoor Classroom Program
R8 / Pacific Southwest Region, California
HQ / National Conservation Training Center, West Virginia

The Schoolyard Habitat/Outdoor Classroom Program (SYH) is a coordinated effort among schools, Service offices, and other conservation and community organizations to establish ecologically sound restoration projects on school sites that function as sustainable outdoor learning areas. With more than 500 Schoolyard Habitat sites throughout the country, the program strongly supports the CPWN priority and the YGO initiative. With Region 8 (California, Nevada, and Klamath Basin) providing the staffing support for national program coordination, the NCTC trains employees and/or partners in the SYH methodology. Region 8, one of the strongest supporter of the program, dedicates six full-time Schoolyard Habitat coordinators who work daily with students, teachers and community volunteers to implement over 20 habitat restoration projects on school grounds each year. The following examples highlight the work of this innovative program in the Service's Pacific Southwest Region.

■ *Capri Elementary School*
Encinitas, Sacramento California.
Kindergartners through sixth graders transformed approximately 1.5 acres of land into native habitat that will double as an Outdoor Learning Lab. This area, once consisting of crab grass, palms, weeds, and other non-native plants, now contains water-wise native California plants that provide food, water, and shelter for butterflies, bugs, small animals, birds, and other wildlife. The project is integrated into Capri's bilingual (English and Spanish) and standard curriculums to encourage long-term environmental stewardship. The environmental education curriculum integrates science, English-language arts, selected children's literature, and student environmental stewardship projects, and prepares students to become future scientists, economists, and green technology leaders. For additional information please see www.fws.gov/FieldNotes/regmap.cfm?arskey=31304&callingKey=region&callingValue=8. For information about other SYH projects in the Sacramento area, see the Capital Public Radio news story on line at www.capradio.org/articles/2012/05/28/garden-program-teaches-kids-and-adults.

■ *Coral Academy of Science, Reno Nevada.*
In 2011 a team from Coral Academy of Science (CAS) elementary school in Reno created a Schoolyard Habitat featuring plants native to the Great Basin and the Sierras. The Schoolyard Habitat at Coral Academy was designed to provide students with the opportunity to connect with nature and observe the interdependency of all living things. CAS has an ongoing interest in the biota of the local ecosystem and hopes that the habitat will specifically provide benefits to pollinators such as bees, butterflies, other insects, and migratory birds. One student, when asked how the habitat will help the environment, responded "It gives out oxygen."

Salmon in the Classroom Program
R1/Columbia River Gorge National Fish
Hatchery Complex, Washington
The Columbia River Gorge National
Fish Hatchery Complex boasts an
extensive and very successful Salmon in
the Classroom Program which provides
a cross-curriculum program for approximately 950 students focused on the daily
development of salmon from eyed egg
to fry life stages. The unit kicks off with
a hatchery tour and culminates with a
fish release field trip where students
watch their fry swim off into the wild.
The hatchery works closely with teachers to ensure the program supports local
academic standards of learning in math,
science, art, and social studies.

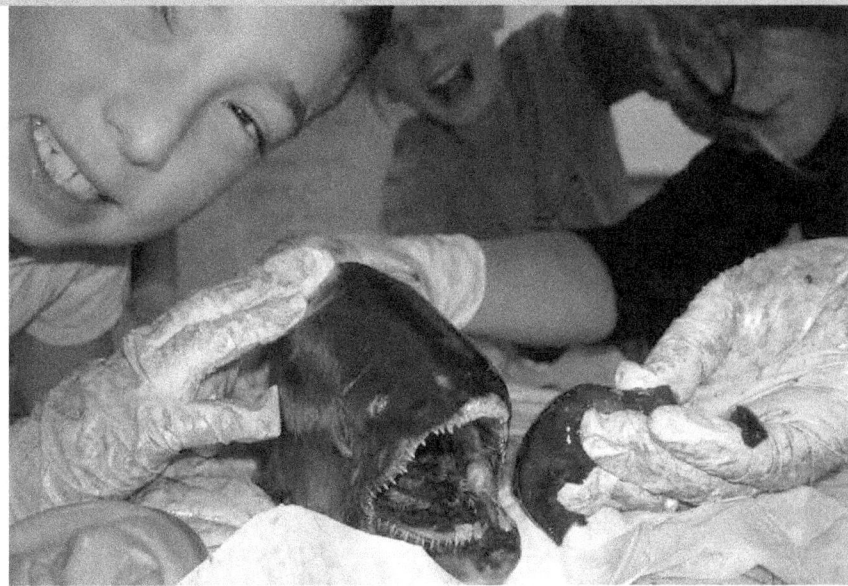

Salmon Dissection

Sac Fry in Fish Tank Gravel

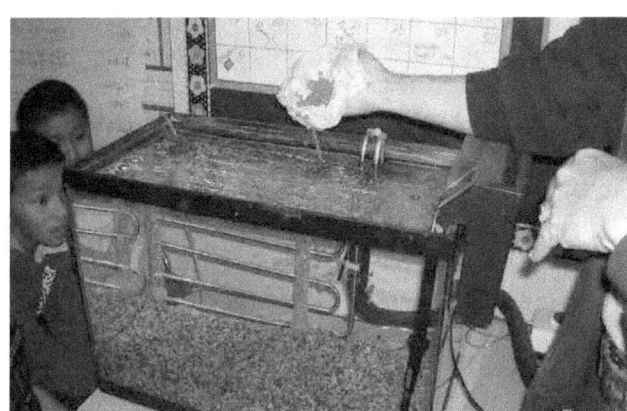

Eggs Going into the Tank

Release Day

Conservation Adventure Camp
R2 / South Texas National Wildlife Refuge Complex, Texas

As a lead in to the high school "Leadership in Nature" camp (see page 17), the South Texas Refuge Complex (Santa Ana, Laguna Atascosa and Lower Rio Grande Valley NWRs) conducted a Conservation Adventure Camp for middle school students. This camp was funded through the RFI (see page 41 for more information on the RFI) and was aimed at introducing middle school students to conservation issues, conservation careers, and fun in the outdoors. Eight middle school students were selected based on applications and essays they had written. During the five-day camp, each day was devoted to exploration of the refuge's big six activities: Monday, hunting with archery and tracking; Tuesday, fishing and angler ethics; Wednesday, photography; Thursday, wildlife observation with birding and kayaking; Friday, interpretation and environmental education with bird banding, tram tour, owl pellet and outdoor investigations; and Saturday, optional family camp out. The grant provided all the materials for the activities, as well as breakfast, lunch, and a snack for all participants, and hats, sunblock, water bottles, insect repellant, backpacks, cameras, binoculars, journals, and field guides for each student.

Archery in the Schools Program
R2 / Southwest Region National Wildlife Refuge System

The Archery in the Schools program has expanded to three of the Region's four states, and now includes the Las Vegas NWR in New Mexico, and Havasu NWR in Arizona. Deep Fork NWR in Oklahoma has supported the program for six years, and it now serves as a warm-up for the students before they go to the state's Archery in the Schools tournament. Students are grouped from grades 4-5 and grades 6-12 for the completion of four stations: a competition shoot, a 3-D animal target-shoot, and a balloon-on-target or a through-rings shoot. The fourth station is rotated each day between a bow fishing station and an Oklahoma Department of Wildlife Conservation Shotgun training education program. The Friends of the Deep Fork NWR provided a pizza lunch for the students and volunteers. Time is also allowed for students to bird watch along the boardwalk during the break. Medals are given out to 1st, 2nd, and 3rd place for both boys and girls, and a team trophy is given to the team that scores the most points.

Native Fish in the Classroom
R2 / New Mexico Fish and Wildlife
Conservation Office

Biologists from the New Mexico Fish and Wildlife Conservation Office are working with several schools on "Native Fish in the Classroom" (NFIC) projects. Modeled after the national Trout in the Classroom program, but with an emphasis on New Mexico native fish species, the program focuses on environmental conservation and includes hands-on classroom activities, presentations, raising fish, and ultimately releasing fish back into their native habitat. NFIC engages students and helps to connect them to real-life water quality, and fish and wildlife issues. NFIC provides standards-based curriculum and fish native to local habitats. Beginning in 2012, one school will be raising red shiner, flathead chub, longnose dace, and river carp sucker; while the remaining three schools will raise Rio Grande cutthroat trout. Participating schools receive all aquaria equipment, local native fish, curriculum, biologist support, and finish the program with a learning trip to release their fish into local native habitat. NFIC crosses all scholastic disciplines and results in stronger understanding of math, science and social studies. Aquariums are up and running in the classrooms and fish will be delivered in January to a total of 12 schools, an increase of four schools. For more information, see www.fws.gov/southwest/fisheries/nmf-wco/education.html

Environmental Education Program
R3 / Alpena Fish and Wildlife Conservation
Office, Michigan

Beginning in 2008, the Alpena Fish and Wildlife Conservation Office implemented a focused outreach program, targeting one group of children at Wilson Elementary School, and following them from grades 2-5. Staff visited their classroom monthly to teach science lessons that coincided with the Michigan Educational Assessment Program (MEAP) curriculum. Lessons provided a lab setting to encourage hands-on learning along with field trips each year to expose the children to a variety of local ecosystems. The intent was to provide students with focused learning opportunities, develop personal relationships, and expose them to a science curriculum that was fun and educational. At the end of the 2012 academic year, the students were assessed by standardized MEAP tests. We were pleasantly surprised to find that this group of children attained the highest MEAP Science scores in Alpena County. The school principal attributed the high scores directly to our classroom involvement, "[these students have] blown away the 5th grade standardized testing in Michigan."

Biologists Andrea Ania and Heather Rawlings teach the Wilson Elementary second grade class about fossils and how they are created.

WoW (Watershed on Wheels) Express
R5 / Silvio O. Conte National Wildlife Refuge, Massachusetts

The WoW Express is a traveling exhibit designed to engage children of all ages in the beauty and wonder of the Silvio O. Conte NWR, which comprises the 7.2 million-acre Connecticut River watershed. The WoW Express includes two engaging components: a walk-through immersion exhibit featuring the diverse sights and sounds of the watershed; and eight, interactive kiosks exploring the cultural, economic, and environmental significance of the Conte NWR. In FY 2012 the WoW Express reached 6,181 people, many of whom may not have otherwise visited a refuge. This represents school children and families in Connecticut, Massachusetts, New Hampshire, and Vermont. The WoW visited 36 schools, 21 of which are in urban communities, reaching 1,140 students in grades 3-6, and 39 teachers. Each program is tailored to the particular school district and complements the state's educational standards. The unique and innovative approach to educating young people about natural resources continues its success and popularity with a full schedule already booked for FY 2013.

Hatchery Helpers
R6 / D.C. Booth Historic National Fish Hatchery, South Dakota

D.C. Booth Historic National Fish Hatchery (NFH) and Archives is home to the Hatchery Helpers Program. This nationally-recognized, award-winning program allows students to learn about nature and conservation through experiences in volunteerism. Youth volunteers complete light maintenance projects such as pulling weeds, watering flowers, painting, and feeding production fish. They also participate in a wildlife conservation and outdoor education program, which includes topics such as electrofishing, bird banding, fly fishing, fish anatomy, and nature journaling. Hatchery Helpers is a fun, free experience in a great learning environment for students entering 6th, 7th, or 8th grade.

DC Booth Historic National Fish Hatchery

Bird Banding Program
R6 / Nebraska Field Office

The Nebraska Ecological Service Field Office partnered with the Iain Nicolson Audubon Center at Rowe Sanctuary to implement a three-week educational bird banding station and a one-day bird banding open house for the general public. A total of 395 high school, middle school, and elementary school students from 11 different schools participated in the bird banding program from September 4-21, 2012. In addition, 24 teachers/adults and one University of Nebraska-Kearney professor attended the banding station. Students rotated through several activity stations including: bird banding; migration headache; migratory mapping; how to use a bird field guide and binoculars; and a bird hike/walk. The Saturday bird banding open house and the three-week bird banding program allowed families and children to have direct experiences in nature. Their experiences included a guided bird hike; observing live birds in the hand via both bird banding and live raptor educational programs; increasing their knowledge about Nebraska's avifauna and the central Platte River; and gaining a better understanding of science as a human endeavor.

Brady High School students taking photos of a Wilson's warbler.

Nature Explore Classroom
HQ / Fish and Aquatic Conservation Program (FAC), Virginia
HQ / National Conservation Training Center, West Virginia

NCTC, FAC, the Creston National Fish Hatchery in Montana, and the Nisqually NWF in Washington State formed a partnership with the Arbor Day Foundation and Dimensions Educational Research Foundation to establish three Nature Explore Classrooms (NEC). NECs are dynamic, nature-based play and learning spaces that use research-based, field-tested design principles. Nisqually NWF was the first Service site to create a NEC. A key component of the NEC projects at NCTC and Creston NFH was the incorporation of youth employment. NCTC's Children's Tree House Child Development Center was built by the Harper's Ferry Job Corps students, and the Northwest Montana Tribal Youth Conservation Corps built the NEC at the Creston NFH. The three Service sites now serve as a model and catalyst for expansion to other Service lands nationwide. To view a video of the NCTC construction project see www.youtube.com/watch?v=F4Xv_SNvaIY

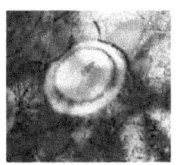

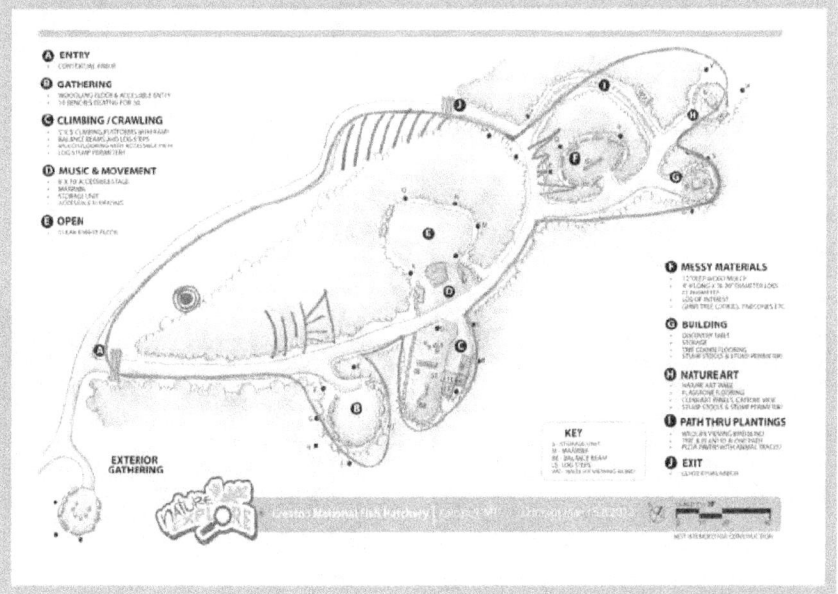

Natural Resource Careers Symposium
HQ / Office of Diversity and Inclusive Workforce Management, Virginia
HQ / National Conservation Training Center, West Virginia

The symposium is a collaborative effort between the Service's Office of Diversity and Inclusive Workforce Management and NCTC's DEO with strong support from nearly all Service programs. The symposium was attended by 80 diverse students, including 58 college students and 22 high school students interested in general science, biology, and environmental disciplines. Attending students represented the following groups: Gates Millennium Scholars; National Hispanic Environmental Council; the University of Maryland (College Park and Eastern Shore campuses); Morgan State University; and Thomas Jefferson High School. The overall goals of the program are: to introduce the students to the Service and its mission, including how the Service addresses key conservation challenges; improve the student's awareness of Service career opportunities; and increase students' knowledge of how to apply for Service internships and permanent jobs.

Sense of Wonder Recognition Program
HQ / National Wildlife Refuge System, Virginia
HQ / National Conservation Training Center, West Virginia

The Sense of Wonder program recognizes Service employees who have designed and implemented visionary programs that foster a sense of wonder and public stewardship of our wildlife heritage. One nominee from each region is selected based on their ability to creatively use the principles of interpretation and environmental education to connect people with nature, especially youth. Sheila McCarten, Visitor Services Manager at the Nisqually NWR Complex in Washington, was selected as the national recipient from the eight regional recipients. Ms. McCarten developed a comprehensive environmental education program which serves as a model for educating children on a large scale on national wildlife refuges. The recipients were recognized at the NAI Workshop in St. Paul, MN.

Shorebird Sister Schools Program (SSSP)
HQ / National Conservation Training Center, West Virginia

A Service international bird curriculum designed to educate K-12 students about the conservation of migratory shorebirds and their habitats, SSSP includes a teacher's guide, student workbooks, posters and a growing website (all materials are available in English and Spanish). In 2012 the program finalized the web publication of an oil spill curriculum which also highlighted a variety of Service careers. www.fws.gov/sssp

Engage

Partnership Programs

Forest Youth Success Program
R1 / Spring Creek National Fish Hatchery, Washington

The Spring Creek National Fish Hatchery partnered with Skamania County Forest Youth Success program to provide necessary maintenance at the hatchery. Forest Youth Success is a summer employment program designed to teach job skills, forest management, ecology, and citizenship and leadership skills to the youth of Skamania County, Washington. The program assists young adults in "learning-by-doing," creating a safe, hands-on learning environment that aims to help enhance life skills and work ethics in young individuals. Students assisted with loading 360 cubic yards of oyster-shell into the hatchery's water reuse system biological filter beds. The labor was done by hand using wheel barrows and rakes. This water filtration system is a critical component of a hatchery system in which 12.2 million tule fall Chinook are reared for spring releases at both Spring Creek (10.5M) and Little White Salmon NFHs (1.7M). To learn more, visit on line at www.fws.gov/gorgefish.

Architecture Construction and Engineering (ACE) Leadership High School Partnership
R2 / Southwest Region Fisheries and Habitat Conservation Program, New Mexico

With the assistance of EDI Architecture, the students at ACE designed, constructed and installed an outdoor education center at the Rio Grande Silvery Minnow Sanctuary which included visitor viewing bridges and informational kiosks. The outdoor area will be used by the community and schools in order to share the importance of ecosystems and endangered species, as well as to connect youth with nature. The students followed all the steps of a real world project by researching and developing kiosk and bridge ideas and models, working with Service engineers and local architects to design ADA compliant structures, and developing a materials and budget list. The students then put their skills to the test and successfully brought their ideas to life by building and installing their structures. Secretary of Labor, Hilda Solis, recently visited ACE High School and recognized the school with a Registered Apprenticeship "Trailblazer and Innovator" Award for its work in preparing young people for careers in high-skilled, hands-on occupations.

Mentoring Weekend for Young Men
R2 / Southwest Region, New Mexico

In June 2012 Dr. Tuggle, the Services' Southeast Regional Director, had the opportunity to join one of Steve Harvey's morning radio shows. The show was broadcast from the Dallas area as part of Harvey's Mentoring Weekend for Young Men. The event provides a one-of-a-kind, empowering experience for young men who are without fathers, and provided over 100 teenage boys from around the country a four-day, three-night transformative weekend. During the interview, Steve Harvey and Dr. Tuggle discussed a variety of issues including the importance of providing youth with the opportunity to experience the outdoors, how the Service engages youth through internships, employment and volunteer opportunities, and the importance of mentoring. After the interview, the Director spent the morning with the young men attending the event and Service staff from a number of programs including fisheries, refuges, law enforcement and ecological services. The staff provided several booths for the young men to visit where they were able to practice casting, learn about fish biology and fish sampling techniques, and see some of the materials that are confiscated by Service law enforcement.

Dr. Tuggle, Southwest Regional Director, and Steve Harvey at the Steve Harvey Mentoring Weekend as they get ready to go fishing.

Lesli Gray/USFWS

St. Louis Art Works Partnership
R3 / Big Muddy National Fish and
Wildlife Refuge (NFWR), Missouri

St. Louis Art Works (www.stlartworks.org) is a non-profit which collaborates with the St. Louis metropolitan area community to provide work experience through apprenticeships in the arts for youth. With grant assistance from the Monsanto Corporation, St. Louis Art Works students visited the Big Muddy NFWR to learn about invasive species. Most of the students in the program have rarely ventured out of inner city St. Louis and were excited about the adventure to the refuge. Located just 14 miles from the heart of the city in the suburb of Chesterfield, the refuge provides a wild retreat in an otherwise urban setting. Using the information gained from these visits, the students will design interpretive signs about invasive species for the refuge. A previous Art Works group designed two interpretive signs about pollinators. One interpretive sign highlights a pollinator garden in the City of Chesterfield and the other educates visitors along a refuge trail.

Students from St. Louis Artworks learn about the Big Muddy National Fish and Wildlife Refuge.

Toes in the Toe Watershed Discovery Program
R4 / Ashville Field Office, North Carolina

Students seldom have the opportunity to spend class time wading rivers or flipping rocks searching for bugs, but during the Toes in the Toe Watershed Discovery, it's actively encouraged. The Toes in the Toe event brings every 5th grade student in North Carolina's mountainous Mitchell and Yancey counties out to a river in their community which is home to an endangered mussel.

During the day, students learn about river health and stewardship, and have the opportunity to explore the river. The event, in its fifth year, is a collaborative effort between the Service and local watershed group Toe River Valley Watch. Stream health in the area is key to the recovery of the endangered Appalachian elktoe mussel. Focusing outdoor environmental education efforts on watersheds with listed species has long been a focus for the Asheville Field Office through this and similar projects.

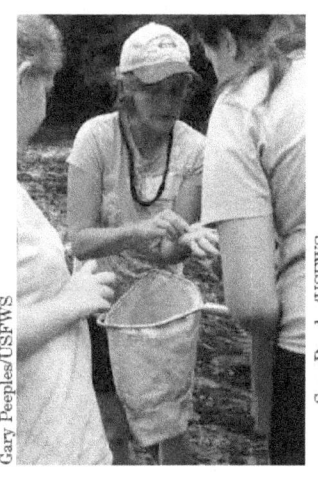

above: A Mitchell County student studies the contents of his net
left: Biologist Andrea Leslie points out a stream insect

Gary Peeples/USFWS

Gary Peeples/USFWS

The Anarchy Zone
R5 / New York Field Office

Children and their families in the greater Ithaca, New York area are getting dirty! The Anarchy Zone, a hands-on nature exploration area has drawn hundreds of children of all ages to explore the outdoors, learn about nature, and have fun while spending time together as families and a community. The Service's New York Field Office collaborated with many organizations including The Ithaca's Children's Garden, Cornell Ornithology Lab and many community volunteers to establish the successful outdoor educational program. The project was funded in part with money from the RFI, and included the innovative use of the social media site Facebook to highlight programs, promote ongoing activities, and provide an avenue for communication. One parent posted the following: "The Anarchy Zone was the highlight of the summer in Ithaca! I have never seen so many children come together before, and have so much fun...expressing themselves and getting dirty, as all children love to do! Wonderful experience for my daughter and a place to encourage children to experience the great outdoors in safety."

Forest L Woods (FLW) Outdoors Foundation Partnership
HQ / Fish and Aquatic Conservation Program (FAC), Virginia

In 2011, the Assistant Director for FAC signed a Memorandum of Understanding (MOU) with FLW Outdoors to provide staff support for the Walmart - FLW Open Tournament 2012 fishing expositions in South Carolina, Missouri, Maryland, Arkansas, New York and Georgia. The main expo received 60,000 attendees alone with each of the other five events averaging 20,000 attendees. At each expo, FAC staff educated participants about the FAC's conservation work and its role in youth engagement, education and employment opportunities.

Living Classrooms of the National Capital Area Partnership
HQ / Fish and Aquatic Conservation Program, Virginia

In May of 2011, the Fisheries Program and the Living Classrooms of the National Capital Region (LCNCR) signed an MOU to engage youth in hands-on outdoor learning experiences. The MOU builds on the relationship with LCNCR that was established in co-sponsoring the annual Nation's River Bass Tournament which introduces over 300 urban youth annually in Washington, DC; Maryland; and Virginia to the vast and historic aquatic resources of the Potomac River. Participants are provided the opportunity to fish with professional bass fishermen and Service volunteers. For the fourth year, Service staff provided educational materials and instructions at three expo booths and provided hands-on instruction in fishing, introducing the sport as a gateway to the great outdoors.

TEDxYouth@Shepherdstown
HQ / National Conservation Training Center, West Virginia

TED is a non-profit dedicated to sharing ideas worth spreading. Originally conceived in a conference format with two sessions per year that involved talks from inspiring leaders lasting no more than 18 minutes, TEDx was designed to give communities, organizations, and individuals the opportunity to stimulate dialog at the local level. NCTC collaborated with two West Virginia Rotary International Clubs to bring TEDx to the Service, for live and taped TED format talks focused on the theme of Connecting Youth to Nature. The ultimate goal was to inspire youth to directly engage with nature, educating themselves about environmental issues and to consider an active lifestyle enjoying and conserving nature. One hundred high school students from five regional institutions participated along with their teachers, parents and Rotary officials. The live talks were professionally videotaped at NCTC and posted on the TEDx website with the potential to reach a wide youth audience. To learn more: www.tedxtalks.ted.com/browse/talks-by-event/tedyouth-shepherdstown

Natural Leaders Network Legacy Camp
HQ / National Conservation Training Center, West Virginia

In partnership with the Children & Nature Network's Natural Leaders Network (NLN), the Service funded a one-week "legacy camp" that provided 24 youth "natural leaders" with communications, community service, and outdoor skills training. Participants were then required to develop an action plan for encouraging people to experience, appreciate, and protect the outdoors in their home communities. Each action plan included activities such as an outdoor service project, a Let's Get Outside event, and a leadership training workshop. The Natural Leaders Network brings together individuals, organizations, and communities, in a non-partisan, inclusive, peer-to-peer network focused on peer-to-peer communication, diversity in nature, and outdoor green jobs.

Nature Champions' Project
HQ / National Conservation Training Center, West Virginia

The Nature Champions Project with the National Environmental Education Foundation finished a two-year pilot in FY 2012. The project, which links Service sites and staff with local doctors and other health care professionals who "prescribe" nature to their adolescent patients, expanded to four Service regions. Various activities include everything from "walks with the Doc" and Nature Yoga, to family campfire sing-a-long programs and animal olympics activities. Thus far, the train-the-trainer model has reached several hundred health care professionals and several thousands of their patients. One of the outcome of the project is highlighted below.

■ *Let's Get Healthy Nature*
  Prescription Program
  R8 / Desert National Wildlife
  Refuge, Nevada
  Southern Nevada Agency
  Partnership (SNAP)
To celebrate Earth Day 2012, patients from the Las Vegas Children's Heart Center (CHC) and their families, 40 people altogether, participated in a stewardship project to improve habitat on the Desert NWR. For the last two years, CHC health care practitioners have been "prescribing nature" to encourage patients go outside and improve their health while connecting with the surrounding natural landscape. Shovels, gloves, seedlings, and buckets of water were ready at the restoration site, and the families jumped right in and got to work. The families were encouraged to return and visit their plants over time to see how well they were doing. The program was also supported with a grant awarded to the Outside Las Vegas Foundation by REI. After lunch, the children were given "Let's Go Outside" whirligig toys, which brought on laughter and active outdoor play for their last memory of the day. More information available from www.fws.gov/FieldNotes/regmap.cfm?arskey=32089&callingKey=region&callingValue=8

Angelina Yost/USFWS

Patients began their adventure with an informational hike on the plants, animals and history of Corn Creek and the Desert National Wildlife Refuge.

Angelina Yost/USFWS

After lunch, the children were given "Let's Go Outside" whirligig toys which brought on laughter and active outdoor play for their last memory of the day.

Agency Programs

Nature Quest Program
R2 / Wichita Mountains National Wildlife Refuge, Oklahoma

Each June underserved students and teachers participate in an interdisciplinary camping program called Nature Quest at the Wichita Mountains NWR. This year 71 grade school students were paired with 15 high school teachers and 15 high school student mentors who spent the week guiding the children through what is, for many, their first time camping or experiencing nature. The first two days children toured the refuge to learn about wildlife conservation, Leave No Trace, healthy lifestyles and safety. The schedule focused on creating bonds between participants, teachers, mentors and staff. On Wednesday, participants hiked nearly three miles to the campground where they pitched their tents, which would be their home for the next two nights. Thursday, the children spent the majority of their time learning to fish or practicing their archery skills. The days are filled with activities, and the nights are also typical camp fun with camp fires, s'mores, storytelling and night hikes. The program also encourages campers and counselors to consider a career in conservation.

Junior Stewards Program
R3 / Upper Mississippi River National Wildlife and Fish Refuge, Minnesota

The refuge's Visitor Services program partnered with the refuge Friends group, Stewards of the Upper Mississippi River NWR, to launch the Junior Stewards program in 2012. Visitor Services manager Ms. Steinhaus commented, "This is the first program I've had where there is a waiting list. The goal is to get these youth outside experiencing the refuge." The purpose of the program is to increase environmental understanding by taking the 16 Junior Stewards and their families out into the prairie once a month to discover insects, grasses, or whatever wildlife happens to be nearby. Junior Stewards also go on canoeing adventures to discover what lies beneath the water's surface. Each participant is assigned a vest, backpack, GPS, camera, binoculars, manuals, and notebook, to journal his findings. Each child chooses a spot on the refuge where he can return each month to observe and record seasonal changes. One student's parent noted, "We know this experience is just the beginning of a lifetime of learning for our son, and could even imagine him some day leading other Junior Stewards or his own children in a similar experience, passing on this awareness and appreciation of nature."

Immersed in the prairie, a Junior Steward journals about his observations.

The 100 degree temperatures in July didn't stop the Junior Stewards and their parents from paddling in the backwaters of the Upper Mississippi River National Wildlife and Fish Refuge.

Junior Stewards discover what lies below the surface during their monthly excursions into the Upper Mississippi River National Wildlife and Fish Refuge.

Junior Stewards at Upper Mississippi River National Wildlife Refuge.

The Wonderland Cave
R4 / Arkansas Field Office

Service biologists at the Arkansas Field Office (AFO) organized a cave clean-up project at the Wonderland Cave in Bella Vista, Arkansas. The Wonderland Cave is cherished by the local community due to its rich historical significance which includes serving as a nightclub, fallout shelter, and a winery. This cave is biologically significant because it provides habitat for many cave-adapted species and is suspected to have supported a colony of federally listed endangered gray bats (*Myotis grisescens*). Unfortunately, the cave was severely vandalized for many years since it was abandoned by previous owners. With permission from the current owner, funding from the RFI, and the help of 75 local residents, students and faculty from Rogers

High School's outdoor education class, members of the Boston Mountain Grotto caving club, and biologists from various state agencies and non-governmental organizations, the AFO coordinated a trash removal day at the delicate cave ecosystem. In addition, student volunteers were educated on cave biology, water quality, endangered species, and White Nose Syndrome (WNS). Upon conclusion of the project, volunteers had completely filled a 20-yard open top dumpster with trash from the cave and had gained valuable knowledge about how to protect sensitive cave ecosystems.

Hatchery Outreach Program
R4 / Private John Allen National Fish Hatchery, Mississippi

The YCC crew of the Private John Allen National Fish hatchery helped the

Hatchery meet its outreach goals for CPWN in FY 2012. This year's crew moved fish and prepared ponds for two major fishing events targeting children age 12 and under. The annual fishing rodeo was once again a huge success with over 200 children and their parents attending this year's event. Pepsi Americas and Wal-Mart continued providing support through donations and refreshments. The YCC crew also assisted hatchery staff in sponsoring a fishing rodeo aimed at providing a recreational fishing experience for handicapped children in the local community. These two events allowed the YCC crew an opportunity to see the importance and become a part of the delivery mechanism for providing community fishing experiences.

Kate Miyamoto / USFWS

On August 10, 2012 the U.S. Fish and Wildlife Service and Partners celebrated the 100 year anniversary of the establishment of the National Elk Refuge. In these photos, young attendees, along with Puddles the Blue Goose and the National Elk Refuge's mascot, showed us how to Get Your Goose On! with style.

Get Your Goose On! Towel Campaign
R6 / National Wildlife Refuge System and External Affairs

To elevate awareness of and appreciation for the NWRS, the Division of Education and Visitor Services and the External Affairs program in the Mountain-Prairie Region developed a campaign called, "Get Your Goose On!" The purpose of the campaign is to engage young people in nature, help them gain an understanding of the Service and the NWRS, and to instill a conservation ethic that may also encourage them to consider working for the Service. For this campaign, a number of "Get Your Goose On!" towels were distributed nationwide. Still and video images were taken of people visiting and working on national wildlife refuges and wetland management districts. Images and video clips are being compiled into a video that will emulate the Pittsburgh Steelers' "Terrible Towel Around the World" commercial. This video will be launched in 2013.

R8 / Desert National Wildlife Refuge

Ten teenagers ages 15-18 from Las Vegas, Pahrump, and Amargosa Valley completed a five-day backpacking trip at Desert NWR. The teens were introduced to Service projects, staff, and resources as a bridge to becoming Natural Leaders within their community. Natural Leaders are young people whose childhood is grounded directly in nature. They inspire others to get outside and advocate experiences that connect youth and children to the outdoors, introducing them to lifestyles of healthy, outdoor activity and environmental stewardship. After backpacking six miles to base camp, the youth learned about backcountry cooking, camping and navigation, cultural history, night life, astronomy, plant identification, animal tracking, radio telemetry techniques, land management, and Leave No Trace ethics. All trip expenses were paid through a Region 8 RFI grant, which allowed the teens to participate for free.

Urban Conservation Treaty for Migratory Birds
HQ / Migratory Bird Program, Arlington

The Urban Conservation Treaty for Migratory Birds (Urban Bird Treaty) program is designed to increase citizen awareness of the importance of migra¬tory birds through partner¬ships between the Service and municipal governments and their partners. Cities work with their partners to conserve migratory birds through education, hazard reductions, citizen science, conservation actions, and conservation and habitat improvement strategies (including restoration of city parks and greenways) in urban/suburban areas. In FY 2012, the pro¬gram reached over 2,000 teachers with bird education workshops designed to engage them in conservation throughout their schools and their communities. Over 23,000 youth in the 19 cities participating in the program were reached with education and outreach programs. Programs such as Christmas Count for Kids introduced bird watching and citizen science to over 500 students.
www.fws.gov/migratorybirds/Partnerships/
UrbanTreaty/urbantreaty.html

Career Awareness Toolkit
HQ / National Conservation Training Center, West Virginia

The DEO developed a Career Awareness Toolkit, which consists of exhibits, lesson plans, and outreach materials to educate and engage elementary to college age students about the variety of careers available within the Service. There are six activities and seven finalized lesson plans available in the toolkit, plus written materials about environmental careers for distribution. The toolkit is designed for all employees, regardless of background, to be able to "grab and go" to career awareness events, such as career fairs and classroom career presentations with little prep time. Two broadcasts are available which offer further details. One is an hour long and the other five minutes. Employees may contact their CPWN Coordinator to have specific items shipped to their field station.
www.distancelearning.fws.gov/players/
careers.html.

Leadership, Coordination, and Training

The Department established the Youth Partnership and Service (YPS) Office to provide Department-wide leadership, coordination, and direction for the YGO initiative. The YPS Office Director reports to the Assistant Secretary for Policy Management and Budget, and the NCTC directly supports the office with permanently assigned staff. The Department also established the YGO Coordinating Council, which consists of executive level bureau representatives, to advise the YGO Office Director. The Chief of the NWRS represents the Service on the Coordinating Council, which meets quarterly and the NCTC Director serves as the Service's alternate. The YGO Task Force was also formed with staff-level bureau and office representatives to support the work of the YPS Office and the Coordinating Council. Representatives from the NWRS, Budget Planning and Human Capital (BPHC), and NCTC regularly attend the monthly YGO Task Force meetings to coordinate work with other Bureaus in the Department. The following activities highlight the important leadership role the Service plays in support of the YGO initiative.

Communications and Reporting

VOICES, (Visitor Outreach, Interpretation, Communication, and Education Services) HQ / National Conservation Training Center, West Virginia

The DEO writes and publishes VOICES, an electronic newsletter published bimonthly to 385 Service employees. Its purpose is to distribute valuable resources for two important initiatives: CPWN and YGO, and topics include educational resources, events, training, conferences, programs, workshops, grants, and awards that will further the growth of Service employees. The colorful email format, with brief write-ups, photos, and videos, features "live" links so Service staff can go directly to the source and further enhance their knowledge. To find archived issues please see http://training.fws.gov/DEO/voices.html

Eddies: Reflections on Fisheries Conservation HQ / Fish and Aquatic Conservation Program

Eddies: Reflections on Fisheries Conservation, is the official quarterly professional journal of the FAC Program. With feature stories and five standing

departments, Eddies is an important tool for communicating the conservation education and youth related work undertaken by the program. FY 2012 included stories such as Jordan River National Fish Hatchery's YCC program and their outdoor classroom enhancement project; Youth Fisheries Academy, a week-long camp connecting Washington State youth to conservation and natural resource careers; and the Native Fish in the Classroom program (see page 25 for more the Native Fish in the Classroom program).

National Conference Support

Supporting and attending national conferences is one of the major ways the Service reaches thousands of people each year with messages about the YGO initiative and our myriad programs that connect people from all walks of life to nature. Following are some of the key events:

- *2011 FFA National Expo HQ / National Conservation Training Center, West Virginia Muscatatuck National Wildlife Refuge, Indiana*
  This event had nearly 55,000 FFA (Future Farmers of America) members and guests in attendance and is one of the largest annual student conventions in the country. NCTC and the Muscatatuck NWR coordinated and staffed the Service's engaging exhibit booth for three days at the Expo to educate participants about the agency's mission and conservation programs, including the Partners with Fish and Wildlife program. Recreational opportunities at refuges and conservation career opportunities were also promoted, and adult advisors were provided materials to teach their students about Service projects and careers.

- *National Association of Interpretation Workshop HQ / National Wildlife Refuge System, Virginia HQ / National Conservation Training Center, West Virginia*
  Employees from the Service participated in this professional workshop about interpretation on November 8-12, 2011, in St. Paul, Minnesota. At an exhibit booth, NCTC employees promoted the

Career Awareness Toolkit, the interagency YouthGo.gov website, and other programs and materials to engage, educate and employ youth. Service employees were also educated about the YGO initiative at the Federal Interagency Council on Interpretation meeting. The national award winner of the Service's Sense of Wonder program was also recognized in a plenary session.

■ *Corps Network Forum*
HQ / National Wildlife Refuge System, Virginia
HQ / National Conservation Training Center, West Virginia
The Corps Network Forum brought together over 200 leaders from 60 different youth development, environmental, and community service organizations to provide youth with job training, academic programming, and leadership skills. The Career Awareness Branch staffed a booth educating participants on conservation careers, the YGO initiative, the YouthGo.gov portal, and displayed items from the Career Awareness Toolkit. Service staff shared information with Corps attendees about the different youth bureau opportunities, internships, and programs.

■ *North American Association for Environmental Education (NAAEE) Annual Conference*
HQ / National Conservation Training Center, West Virginia
With 25 employees in attendance, the NAAEE conference is the most heavily attended conference of the year in support of the YGO initiative and CPWN priority. Employees teamed up with our partners to propose ten papers, all of which were accepted for presentation at the conference. Additionally, the Service staffed a booth at the conference to share our innovative materials and programs with conference attendees. NCTC organized and held a Service employee meeting to better coordinate our efforts, share best practices, and identify strategies for NCTC to better support environmental education at the field level.

Let's Go Outside Website
HQ / National Conservation Training Center, West Virginia
As part of the CPWN priority, the "Let's Go Outside" (LGO) website is a dynamic resource for children, parents, educators, and youth group leaders. The site encourages its audience to go outside and connect with nature, learn about the environment and conservation, and develop a greater appreciation of the Service including volunteer opportunities and Service careers. A wide-range of topics with links to other websites for each audience group includes visiting Refuges - parents and children; creating schoolyard habitats - educators; and planning outdoor trips - youth group leaders. Content is refreshed several times a year.
www.fws.gov/letsgooutside

Youth Trac
HQ / National Conservation Training Center, West Virginia
HQ / National Wildlife Refuge System
HQ / Budget Planning and Human Capital Youth Coordination Team

The Service established the Youth Coordination Team (YCT), with representatives from each region and HQ program office, to help increase the number and diversity of youth (ages 15-25) entering into natural resources and cultural heritage public service jobs (see page 42 for more on the YCT). In response to new reporting requirements issued by the Department in December 2011 for the Secretary's Youth Priority Performance Goal (PPG), the Service established and piloted the first agency-wide partnership employment reporting tool called Youth Trac. This new tool will enable the agency to track demographic trends for all youth the Service employs through partnership agreements each year, and in combination with the Federal Personnel and Payroll System (FPPS), will expand the capacity for monitoring progress at achieving diversity goals.

Coordination

YouthGo Web Portal
HQ / National Conservation Training Center, West Virginia

Under the NCTC's leadership, the Department's bureaus collectively outlined the vision and design of the YouthGo Web Portal, which provides a professional networking platform for young people seeking employment to share information on their career interests, educational backgrounds, and work experiences. As a result, the portal is now increasingly being viewed by managers as a feeder resource for new recruits. In 2012, the Department partnered with the U.S. Forest Service to expand the portal and is currently piloting a tool that will allow agencies to record, monitor, track, and certify student intern hours worked in fulfillment of the non-competitive eligibility requirements outlined in the Public Land Service Corps Hiring Authority. The new tracking module will be online for use in the 2013

hiring season. Since the portal's launch, the site has received nearly 68,000 visits and more than 313,000 page views, with visitors spending an average of nearly 10 minutes on the site. To learn more go to www.youthgo.gov

Fisheries Conservation Education Program
HQ / Fish and Aquatic Conservation

The National Fisheries Education Team, which consists of a coordinator in each region, continues to increase opportunities to engage, educate, and employ youth at fisheries facilities, and to improve accomplishment reporting. This year, the Team developed a Fisheries Program Conservation Education Strategy with guidance for utilizing the strategy and associated tasks.

Connecting People with Nature
HQ / National Conservation Training Center, West Virginia

The Connecting People with Nature (CPWN) National Working Group coordinates connecting people with nature activities that engage and educate families, educators, students, and youth groups, and develops career awareness programs. CPWN is the foundation of the YGO initiative. The CPWN National Working Group was established in 2007 as a result of a Service Directorate priority, and is comprised of regional and HQ program representatives that hold monthly conference calls and an annual meeting. Priorities include the development and management of the Let's Go Outside website (www.letsgooutside. gov), and the RFI which provides critically important financial resources to the Service's field stations and regional offices for innovative projects that engage and educate pre-high school aged youth and their educators.

Connecting People with Nature National Working Group Membership

Region 1	Nancy Pollot	nancy_pollot@fws.gov
Region 2	Art Needleman	art_a_needleman@fws.gov
Region 3	Tim Smigielski	tim_smigielski@fws.gov
Region 4	Garry Tucker	garry_tucker@fws.gov
Region 5	Jennifer Lapis	jennifer_lapis@fws.gov
Region 6	Dee Emmons	diane_emmons@fws.gov
Region 7	Cathy Rezabeck	cathy_rezabeck@fws.gov
Region 8	DC Carr	derrick_carr@fws.gov
Headquarters		
Endangered Species		
	Lew Gorman	lewis_gorman@fws.gov
Fish and Aquatic Conservation		
	Denise Wagner	denise_wagner@fws.gov
Law Enforcement	Sharon Lynn	sharon_lynn@fws.gov
Migratory Birds	Rachel Levin	rachel_levin@fws.gov
National Conservation Training Center		
	Mary Danno	mary_danno@fws.gov
National Wildlife Refuge System		
	Marcia Pradines	marcia_pradines@fws.gov
	Nathan Caldwell	nathan_caldwell@fws.gov

Youth Coordination Team
HQ / National Conservation Training Center, West Virginia

The Youth Coordination Team (YCT) is focused on the coordination of employment programs and activities for youth aged 15 – 25. Key programs include YCC, Pathways (formerly SEEP), and youth employed through partnerships. With representatives from every region and most HQ programs, the group meets monthly on conference calls to coordinate departmental reporting requirements, share strategies for increasing the number of youth employed each year, and provide advice and input to the development of departmental policy initiatives such as the new YCC handbook.

Youth Program Policy
HQ / National Conservation Training Center, West Virginia

NCTC is coordinating a comprehensive effort to revise the Service Manual to ensure that the YGO initiative is appropriately codified in Service policy. Key to this effort is drafting and publishing a new chapter that establishes a framework for youth programming from the field to regional and HQ offices; outlines the wide variety of complementary programs and opportunities through which employees may engage, educate, and employ youth, partners, and volunteers; describes the overall roles and responsibilities of our employees related to the youth program; and identifies and links to youth engagement, education, and employment program policies in other sections of the Service Manual so that employees can see the entire spectrum of relevant policy. With these revisions to Service policy the YGO initiative is firmly positioned for long-term success.

Training

HQ / National Conservation Training Center, West Virginia

The DEO has the lead for the development and implementation of professional development training for Department employees and their partners responsible for the YGO initiative. Key training strands and courses are described below. Courses are offered in face-to-face and distance-learning formats.

- *The Youth Outdoor Skills Curriculum Strand* offers five courses that provide Service employees with skills and tools that they can use to actively engage youth in the outdoors. This year an additional 22 participants graduated from the course *Archery as an Outreach Tool* which provided instructor certification to Service and State agency personnel to teach youth archery as a sport or for hunting. Archery not only requires discipline, motor skills, patience, and a desire to have fun, but also links youth to the outdoors, conservation, and career opportunities.

- *The Environmental Education Curriculum Strand* offers 18 courses that focus on best practices and demonstrate how environmental education serves as a resource management tool for the Service. In FY 2012 the *Creating a Schoolyard Habitat/Outdoor Classroom* course was offered in two locations to help Service employees develop tools to conserve habitat necessary to local native species while providing environmental education experiences to school-age children and their teachers. Through innovative partnerships and creative problem solving, the Service is creating outdoor classrooms that both advance the agency's mission and provide a learning laboratory for our nation's youth. Schoolyard habitat engages and educates students and teachers about conservation by providing lasting, meaningful and place-based outdoor educational experiences at community schools.

Youth Coordination Team Membership

Region 1	Robert Peyton	bob_peyton@fws.gov
Region 2	Gary Hutchison	gary_hutchison@fws.gov
Region 3	Ann Marie Chapman	annmarie_chapmen@fws.gov
Region 4	Sharon Fuller	sharon_fuller@fws.gov
Region 5	Jennifer Lapis	jennifer_lapis@fws.gov
Region 6	Dee Emmons	diane_emmon s@fws.gov
Region 7	Kristen Gilbert	kristen_gilbert@fws.gov
Region 8	Dara Rodriguez	dara_rodriguez@fws.gov
Headquarters		
Diversity Inclusive Workforce Management		
	Bill Farr	bill_farr@fws.gov
Endangered Species		
	Martha Balis-Larsen	martha_balislarsen@fws.gov
Fish and Aquatic Conservation		
	Robert Pos	robert_pos@fws.gov
Human Capital Management		
	Kelly Billote	kelly_billote@fws.gov
Migratory Birds	Alicia King	alicia_king@fws.gov
National Conservation Training Center		
	Drew Burnett	drew_burnett@fws.gov
National Wildlife Refuge System		
	Phil LePelch	phil_lepelch@fws.gov

■ *The Youth Leadership and Supervision Curriculum Strand* offers four courses for Service and Department supervisors and team leaders who work directly with the younger employees, providing them with tools and resources to solve complex environmental and natural resource problems using management strategies that will work most effectively and productively for them. This year, a new self-paced online course, *Mentoring: Getting Started with your Mentee*, was launched to help employees support, motivate, guide and encourage their mentees as they seek to achieve their career and education goals.

■ *Championing Diversity* courses instructed by Franklin Covey were offered at NCTC, Region 3, and HQ to approximately 100 employees. These dynamic courses instructed participants in how to improve on their ability to lead and work effectively as they strive for excellence and diversity in the workplace. Participants learned how to understand diversity, then actively seek out and leverage differences in order to achieve better, sustained results. Understanding diversity is vitally important as the Service addresses an employee retirement wave with strategies for filling the resulting vacancies with more diverse employees.

■ *Service Employee Foundations* course is required training for all employees and it is offered quarterly at NCTC. With class sizes typically reaching 30 students, DEO developed and integrated a presentation that provides an overview of the YGO initiative, why it is important for achieving the Service's mission, and how the agency is coordinating efforts through the CPWN National Working Group and YCT to improve the quality of our programs and increase the number of youth the Service reaches each year. Of the more than 120 employees participating this year, many incorporated youth components in their work.

■ *Summer Pathways* is a partnership effort among DEO and HQ program offices. The program helped 28 HQ summer interns learn about the broad array of Service and Department career opportunities available, and begin developing professional networks across a variety of career specialties. The program consisted of six brown bag lunch speakers from various program areas and three off-site field trips to the Main Interior Building, NCTC, and Patuxent Research Refuge. The brown bag speakers inspired the interns to learn more about the Service and various natural resource career options. Post-experience surveys indicated the interns thought the Service should provide the program next summer. Not surprisingly the field trips were the highlight of the program, and the coordinator recommends incorporating a service learning component into next year's syllabus.

Conclusion

This report demonstrates how deeply integrated youth programs are throughout the Service, from field stations, fish hatcheries, and national wildlife refuges, to regional and national program offices. As the Service confronts the increasing wave of employee retirements and decreasing interest in the outdoor environment among our nation's young people, the importance of building the next generation of conservation leaders to join our ranks and tackle complex conservation challenges becomes all the more important. The Service is proud of the comprehensive nature of our programs that reach millions of young people, their educators, and their families every year. We engage children while they are young, we educate them as they grow, and we offer exciting job opportunities when they are ready to enter the working world as adults. We look forward to improving our programs and sharing our experiences more broadly, always with the hope of involving more young people in the important work we do: working with people to conserve, protect and enhance fish, wildlife, plants and their habitats for the continuing benefit of the American people.

U.S. Department of the Interior
U.S. Fish & Wildlife Service

http://www.fws.gov

Federal Relay
1 800/877 8339 Voice and TTY

March 2013

www.ingramcontent.com/pod-product-compliance
Lightning Source LLC
Chambersburg PA
CBHW081125280526
45787CB00007B/2988

9 781507 769881